No More

Live Free!

A Guide to Identifying and
Overcoming Anxiety

MARIE L. LAWSON

WESTBOW
PRESS®
A DIVISION OF THOMAS NELSON
& ZONDERVAN

This book is a work of non-fiction. Unless otherwise noted, the author and the publisher make no explicit guarantees as to the accuracy of the information contained in this book and in some cases, names of people and places have been altered to protect their privacy.

WestBow Press books may be ordered through booksellers or by contacting:

WestBow Press
A Division of Thomas Nelson & Zondervan
1663 Liberty Drive
Bloomington, IN 47403
www.westbowpress.com
844-714-3454

Because of the dynamic nature of the Internet, any web addresses or links contained in this book may have changed since publication and may no longer be valid. The views expressed in this work are solely those of the author and do not necessarily reflect the views of the publisher, and the publisher hereby disclaims any responsibility for them.

Any people depicted in stock imagery provided by Getty Images are models, and such images are being used for illustrative purposes only.
Certain stock imagery © Getty Images.

Scripture quotations marked (NIV) are taken from the Holy Bible, New International Version®, NIV®. Copyright © 1973, 1978, 1984, 2011 by Biblica, Inc.™ Used by permission of Zondervan. All rights reserved worldwide. www.zondervan.com The "NIV" and "New International Version" are trademarks registered in the United States Patent and Trademark Office by Biblica, Inc.™

Scripture taken from the New King James Version®. Copyright © 1982 by Thomas Nelson. Used by permission. All rights reserved.

ISBN: 978-1-6642-1538-2 (sc)
ISBN: 978-1-6642-1537-5 (e)

Library of Congress Control Number: 2020924096

Print information available on the last page.

WestBow Press rev. date: 01/22/2021

Contents

To my family:

My dearest mother who loves me so wonderfully, my sisters and brothers, and my

beautiful nieces and awesome nephews. Thank you for your love and support.

To my friends who are all reflections of God's love to me.

Bless you all!

Anxiety weighs down the heart, but a kind word cheers it up.

—Proverbs 12:25 (NIV)

Introduction

This book is based on the processes I've used in my counseling sessions, and some are from my own experience. Seeing the results led me to writing this book as a guide to helping people struggling with anxiety.

Our lives are busy, and there are a number of stressors bound to cause anxiety, including increased shootings, the state of world affairs, calamities, and catastrophes. Anxiety keeps us from living fully. It leads to sickness and behaviors that affect everything, such as work, the joy of living, and everyone around us and close to us, such as our families.

We have heard in the news that anxiety disorders are the most common mental illness in the United States, affecting over forty million people aged eighteen and older according to Anxiety and Depression Association of America (Ritchie and Roser 2018). This illness is treatable; I have been able to do so in my practice. Yet the percentage of people getting help is at a record low. That means we are sick and living life at risk.

There is hope for each person struggling with anxiety. I believe that anyone who follows the simple steps in this book will see results and be on the way to wellness and peace.

We are called to abundant life in Christ. John 10:10b (NKJV) states, "I have come that they might have life, and that they might have it more abundantly."

You are valuable! You have a purpose and destiny to fulfill, so let's get free!

What Is Making You Anxious?

Have you ever stopped to consider the things in your life that cause you to be excessively uneasy or apprehensive and result in compulsive actions or panic attacks? Perhaps for you it may not be as severe as a panic attack. Maybe it's that subtle undercurrent of fear you recognize when faced with certain situations.

However subtle or severe the symptoms of anxiety can be, Philippians 4:6 tells us how to handle our anxious moments. It reads, "Do not be anxious about anything, but in every situation, by prayer and petition, with thanksgiving, present your requests to God." If you are not allowing God to control your life and direct your path, anxiety will be a constant companion.

> **Know this: You're not alone. Help is available!**

Prayer is a part of my practice; I pray for all my clients until I see results. I believe in the power of prayer, and I incorporated it in this guide because of the results. I remember in one session my client was having severe attacks and seemed to be getting worse with each session. After waiting in prayer, praying with the family, and opening and closing each session with a prayer, the breakthrough came within a matter of weeks. Prayer then became a part of my client's family life.

Perception of God

Your view of God affects your ability to give Him complete control. If you grew up with an abusive or controlling father, chances are that you won't trust God with your life.

What is your view of God? Is He dependable, reliable, trustworthy, and a friend? If you can see Him as your heavenly Father, one who loves you beyond the way anyone on earth can, you can't help but give Him control. You will want to give Him every area of your life because He knows what's best for you! He created you. His love is patient and kind, and He is not easily angered. He keeps no record of your wrongs. He protects. He can be trusted with all that is making you anxious. Our Father cares. His gifts are much more than any earthly father could give to you (Matthew 7:11 NIV).

When anxiety affects your state of being, your day-to-day life, and people around you, you need to take immediate action.

> Know this: Your life is a gift.

Your life is a gift, and learning to enjoy a life free of anxiety is possible. Be determined to seek help through counseling and support from your family and church.

What Causes Anxiety?

Anxiety is the result of the brain's inability to produce and regulate GABA (gamma-aminobutyric acid), which is a neurotransmitter that blocks impulses between nerve cells in the brain. It is an amino acid produced naturally in the brain. It facilitates communication among brain cells and serotonin, which is an important chemical and neurotransmitter in the human body. It is believed to help regulate mood and social behavior, appetite and digestion, sleep, memory, and sexual desire and function.

> **Know this: You are fearfully and wonderfully made (Psalm 139:14).**

The following are some contributing factors to anxiety.

- environmental factors
- stress
- job
- school
- finances
- traumatic events
- heights
- genetics
- medication, disease, long-term medical conditions
- brain chemistry
- use of illegal substances

- poor diet

- unresolved childhood issues

Anxiety can be severe. More than forty million people in the United States suffer from anxiety. The increasing incidents of this mental disorder are concerning but not surprising when you consider the world we live in. Life today can produce a daily dose of traumas and fears. But only a small percentage of people with anxiety get the help they need to cope with and overcome the problem.

Anxiety can be overwhelming. It can feel like a thick cloud, a wall, or darkness. It can control every step a person takes and every decision he or she makes.

Interestingly, anxiety is not always harmful. It can be protective. God created our bodies to respond to danger by taking evasive action. Our response to impending danger can come in the form of an increased heartbeat, sweating, and a heightened awareness of our surroundings. It can create a rush of adrenaline. This is called the flight-or-fight response, a natural reaction to confront or flee danger. Again, anxiety is normal and necessary for survival when facing approaching dangers or worrying triggers.

Trigger Story

The last time I saw my abusive boyfriend, he had on a bright orange shirt and blue jeans. Every time I saw a man who resembled him in those clothes, it caused fear to arise in me. I became paranoid and thought he was close by.

To escape the harmful type of anxiety, you must be able to grasp it. Once you become aware of your feelings and the behavior that is causing the physical symptoms, then you can get help to manage the symptoms and prevent anxiety from overtaking your life. Identifying what you are feeling is an important step to a breakthrough.

Common Symptoms

Symptoms are clues to let you know something is wrong that could lead to something more severe. Pay attention to the following list. If you are experiencing any of them, it's time to take action.

- dizziness
- trembling
- back pain
- sweating
- being easily startled
- muscle tension
- restlessness and fatigue
- increased or irregular heartbeat
- ongoing worry without a trigger
- clinical depression
- decreased energy
- heart palpitations
- smothering sensations
- difficulty breathing
- desire to escape
- abdominal discomfort

- hot or cold flashes

- feeling of choking

- nightmares

Note that multiple symptoms can show up at the same time.

Types of Anxiety Disorders

Generalized Anxiety Disorder (GAD)

https://www.medicalnewstoday.com/articles/323454

More than three million cases of GAD occur every year in the United States, according to a Mayo Foundation for Medical Education and Research study (1998–2010). It is common in children and teenagers and very common in adults. Some things to note:

- GAD is a chronic disorder involving excessive, long-lasting anxiety and worries about nonspecific life events, objects, and situations.
- It is the most common anxiety disorder.
- GAD is not easily identified.
- According to the American Psychological Association (APA), someone with GAD may require professional help if he or she has recurring, intrusive thoughts or concerns.

Obsessive-Compulsive Disorder (OCD)

OCD affects 2.2 million people in the United States.

This anxiety disorder is characterized by thoughts or actions that are repetitive, distressing, and intrusive. People with OCD usually know that their compulsions are unreasonable or irrational, but they serve to alleviate their anxieties. Those with OCD may obsessively clean personal items and body parts, like hands, or constantly check locks, stoves, or light switches.

Panic Disorder (PD)

Some three million people in the United States have PD (*Psychology Today* 2016). Brief or sudden attacks of intense terror and apprehension characterize panic disorder. These attacks can lead to shaking, confusion, dizziness, nausea, and breathing difficulties.

Panic attacks tend to occur and escalate rapidly and then peak after ten minutes. But they can last for hours. This disorder occurs after frightening experiences or prolonged stress but can also occur without a trigger.

An individual experiencing an attack may misinterpret it as a life-threatening illness. Panic attacks can also lead to drastic changes in behavior to avoid future attacks.

Phobia Anxiety Disorder

Around nineteen million adults in the United States suffer from phobia anxiety disorder (Ritchie and Roser 2018). Some things to note:

- This is an irrational fear and avoidance of an object or situation.
- Phobias differ from other anxiety disorders, as they relate to a specific cause.
- The fear may be acknowledged as irrational or unnecessary, but the person is still unable to control the anxiety.
- Triggers for a phobia may be as varied as situations, animals, or everyday objects.

Posttraumatic Stress Disorder (PTSD)

According to the Calm Clinic, seven million people were living with or experiencing PTSD in 2017.

This anxiety results from previous trauma such as military combat, sexual assault, a hostage situation, or a serious accident. PTSD often leads to flashbacks, and the person with PTSD may make behavioral changes to avoid triggers.

Separation Anxiety Disorder

More than two hundred thousand cases of separation anxiety disorder occur in the United States every year. It's common in babies and children up to age fourteen.
(Ritchie and Roser 2018).

This is characterized by high levels of anxiety when separated from a person or place that provides feelings of security or safety. Separation sometimes results in panic symptoms. It is considered a disorder when the response is excessive or inappropriate after separation.

Social Anxiety Disorder

Approximately fifteen million adults in the United States have a social anxiety disorder, usually starting in the teenage years (Ritchie and Roser 2018).

This is a fear of being negatively judged by others in a social situation or a fear of intimacy or humiliation. This disorder can cause people to avoid public situations and human contact to the point that everyday living is rendered extremely difficult.

Early Intervention

As with most things in life, the longer you wait to get help for anxiety, the longer it could take to see results. If you are experiencing anxiety, seek help right away. Here are some steps to get started. These actions that can bring immediate results and become a lifestyle.

- Keep a diary or journal. Writing down your thoughts, feelings, and daily activities can be helpful. This is one way to release your feelings. (Example journal prompt: Write about an event that caused you to smile.)
- Managing your time and keeping a record of important information can help lessen stress, give you a visual of each task and spending, and an idea of what to expect to minimize feeling overwhelmed. (A notebook or app can be a good way to track each purchase.)

Be aware of your personality and temperament. Assessments are available to help with understanding yourself. Knowing how God made you can help you live freely. This has helped many of my clients. Knowing when to engage, when to be alone, and when to rest has helped me balance how I spend my time. How you spend your time should be evaluated to avoid anxiety.

Treatment

Treatments for anxiety include physical examinations, medication, and Christ-centered behavioral therapy counseling. Sometimes underlying conditions must be brought under control before treating the disorder.

Managing stress is also an important tool in treating anxiety. Here are some ways to manage stress:

- Relaxation—Get in the habit of taking four hours weekly to do nothing.

- Exercise—Find exercises that will help you to stretch and relax; simply taking long walks can be so helpful as a starter. You can also find a personal trainer and group exercises.

- Listen to music—Find something relaxing and uplifting, such as instrumental or jazz.

- Positive thoughts—Replace negative thoughts with God's promises.

- Support groups—Care groups at community centers and churches can be helpful.

- Hobbies—Try hobbies such as sewing, running, fishing, and a reading club.

- Healthy diet—Follow a healthy meal plan that works for your budget and reduce fast foods.

- Establish a regular sleep pattern—Try to get to bed at a set time each night.

- Use pure essential oils—Oils such as lavender have therapeutic properties. Note: Use with caution and follow instructions.

- Avoid alcohol and other recreational drugs: Things to be avoided include diet sodas, MSG, corn syrup, coffee, nondairy creamer, and beef jerky.

- Daily Bible reading—See the thirty-day plan in this book to jump-start your journey to being free from anxiety.

- Continuous prayer—Be persistent in prayer until you see results. Join prayer groups, start prayer alters, and be consistent by making prayer a priority each day.

- Anxiety medication—Medications can be helpful, but beware of the side effects of antidepressants, benzodiazepines, buspirone, tricyclics, beta-blockers, and monoamine oxidase inhibitors (MAOIs). Please discuss these with your doctor.

- Don't give up!

> **Know This**
> **Nothing is impossible.**
> **—God (Luke 1:37 NIV)**

A Thirty-Day Plan to Overcoming Anxiety

List the following according to categories in as much detail as possible. This should continue for approximately thirty days. Consistency and commitment are important to achieving optimum results. Get an accountability partner if necessary to check in with throughout this plan.

Day 1

Foods/Meals

_____

Activities/Exercise

_____

Hours of sleep

_____

Symptom

_____

Discovery:

Day 2

Foods/Meals

_____

Activities/Exercise

_____

Hours of sleep

_____

Symptom

_____

Discovery:

Day 3

Foods/Meals

_____

Activities/Exercise

_____

Hours of sleep

_____

Symptom

_____

Discovery:

Day 4

Foods/Meals

_____

Activities/Exercise

_____

Hours of sleep

_____

Symptom

_____

Discovery:

Day 5

Foods/Meals

_____

Activities/Exercise

_____

Hours of sleep

_____

Symptom

_____

Discovery:

Day 6

Foods/Meals

_____

Activities/Exercise

_____

Hours of sleep

_____

Symptom

_____

Discovery:

Day 7

Foods/Meals

_____

Activities/Exercise

_____

Hours of sleep

_____

Symptom

_____

Discovery:

Day 8

Foods/Meals

_____

Activities/Exercise

_____

Hours of sleep

_____

Symptom

_____

Discovery:

Day 9

Foods/Meals

_____

Activities/Exercise

_____

Hours of sleep

_____

Symptom

_____

Discovery:

Day 10

Foods/Meals

_____

Activities/Exercise

_____

Hours of sleep

_____

Symptom

_____

Discovery:

Day 11

Foods/Meals

_____

Activities/Exercise

_____

Hours of sleep

_____

Symptom

_____

Discovery:

Day 12

Foods/Meals

_____

Activities/Exercise

_____

Hours of sleep

_____

Symptom

_____

Discovery:

Day 13

Foods/Meals

_____

Activities/Exercise

_____

Hours of sleep

_____

Symptom

_____

Discovery:

Day 14

Foods/Meals

_____

Activities/Exercise

_____

Hours of sleep

_____

Symptom

_____

Discovery:

Day 15

Foods/Meals

_____

Activities/Exercise

_____

Hours of sleep

_____

Symptom

_____

Discovery:

Day 16

Foods/Meals

_____

Activities/Exercise

_____

Hours of sleep

_____

Symptom

_____

Discovery:

Day 17

Foods/Meals

_____

Activities/Exercise

_____

Hours of sleep

_____

Symptom

_____

Discovery:

Day 18

Foods/Meals

_____

Activities/Exercise

_____

Hours of sleep

_____

Symptom

_____

Discovery:

Day 19

Foods/Meals

_____

Activities/Exercise

_____

Hours of sleep

_____

Symptom

_____

Discovery:

Day 20

Foods/Meals

_____

Activities/Exercise

_____

Hours of sleep

_____

Symptom

_____

Discovery:

Day 21

Foods/Meals

_____

Activities/Exercise

_____

Hours of sleep

_____

Symptom

_____

Discovery:

Day 22

Foods/Meals

Activities/Exercise

Hours of sleep

Symptom

Discovery:

Day 23

Foods/Meals

_____

Activities/Exercise

_____

Hours of sleep

_____

Symptom

_____

Discovery:

Day 24

Foods/Meals

_____

Activities/Exercise

_____

Hours of sleep

_____

Symptom

_____

Discovery:

Day 25

Foods/Meals

_____

Activities/Exercise

_____

Hours of sleep

_____

Symptom

_____

Discovery:

Day 26

Foods/Meals

_____

Activities/Exercise

_____

Hours of sleep

_____

Symptom

_____

Discovery:

Day 27

Foods/Meals

Activities/Exercise

Hours of sleep

Symptom

Discovery:

Day 28

Foods/Meals

_____

Activities/Exercise

_____

Hours of sleep

_____

Symptom

_____

Discovery:

Day 29

Foods/Meals

_____

Activities/Exercise

_____

Hours of sleep

_____

Symptom

_____

Discovery:

Day 30

Foods/Meals

_____

Activities/Exercise

_____

Hours of sleep

_____

Symptom

_____

Discovery:

List Anxiety

This will give you clues as to who else in the family may have an anxiety issue and how to treat the illness.

In Family (F)

In Self (S)

List	Self	Family

Exposing the Root Response

Exposing the root helps allow the healing to take place by identifying the right responses versus the wrong responses. This could bring quick results when the root is exposed and addressed.

I am anxious over …	
I was embarrassed when …	
I felt abandoned …	
I was hurt when …	
I will never let it happen again.	

Helping Your Body to Relax

Train your brain to focus on something pleasurable by closing your eyes and thinking a happy thought for five minutes. Increase daily until you reach thirty minutes.

Inhale and exhale, and count to ten. Repeat as necessary to relax.

Stretch.

Tighten fingers and toes and then release. Do this for five minutes or as needed to relax. This can be done from a standing position or while lying on a mat.

Food/Supplement List

Studies have shown that a healthy, balanced diet can help to bring healing to your body. The following is a list of some foods and supplements known to help decrease anxiety. Organic foods and supplements are recommended.

- almonds
- asparagus
- vitamin B6
- bananas
- blueberries
- chamomile
- holy basil Tulsi tea
- green tea
- peppermint tea or extract
- chia seeds
- cinnamon
- citrus fruit and bell peppers
- dark chocolate
- eggs

- herbs such as valerian
- leafy greens, spinach, swiss chard, sprouts
- meat and dairy products
- nuts
- oats
- omega 3
- probiotics
- salmon
- seeds
- turkey
- turmeric
- whole grains
- yogurt
- water

Consult a dietary handbook for more detailed advice.

You're Not Alone

At some point in life, everyone will experience anxiety. That's just how we are made. So get this in your mind: You are not alone. Help is available when anxiety begins to affect your daily life and the lives of those around you. Seek out friends, family, and your church congregation. Take advantage of Christian counseling services. And consider a physical examination.

For more information and resources, or to schedule an appointment, please visit preparedapproach.com.

Thirty Days to Freedom Devotional

Scriptures, Prayers, and Meditations for Each Day

This devotional is designed to work in the order of body, soul, and spirit to get results. We are three-part beings, and I find if I work with clients in a way that addresses all three parts, the results come much quicker. Again it will take work and consistency to see results. Everyone is different. Be patient and do the work. It can be helpful to work with a friend, spouse, or family member who wants to help you handle anxiety in a healthy way.

Spiritual Growth

To overcome anxiety, the Scriptures, with prayer, is a way to jump-start your own prayer time.

Open Prayer

Jesus, come into my heart. Forgive me of my sin. Be my Lord and Savior. Give me grace to forgive others and myself. Take control of my life. I thank you for the gift of salvation.

Heavenly Father, I desire to be fully healed of anxiety and to be restored to fulfill my potential. As I go through this devotional and gain understanding, teach me how to know your voice and what applies to me, along with my underlying false belief system. Thank you, Jesus, for dying on the cross to make a way for my freedom. In the mighty name of Jesus Christ, I Pray. Amen!

Read John 14:25–27 (NIV)

All this I have spoken while still with you. But the Advocate, the Holy Spirit, whom the Father will send in my name, will teach you all things and will remind you of everything I have said to you. Peace I leave with you; my peace I give you. I do not give to you as the world gives. Do not let your hearts be troubled and do not be afraid.

Prayer: I receive the peace of God that dispels anxiety. Holy Spirit, fill me with Your peace. Amen

Journal Highlights and Thoughts throughout This Process

2 DAY

Read Isaiah 41:10 (NIV)

So do not fear, for I am with you; do not be dismayed, for I am your God. I will strengthen you and help you; I will uphold you with my righteous right hand.

Prayer: Thank You, God, for helping me not to fear and holding me with Your righteous right hand. In Jesus's name, I will not fear. Amen.

Read Isaiah 43:1 (NIV)

But now, this is what the Lord says, He who created you, Jacob, He who formed you, Israel: "Do not fear, for I have redeemed you; I have summoned you by name; you are mine."

Prayer: Thank You, Jesus, for justifying, sanctifying, atoning for, and redeeming me. You are mine, and I am Yours. I believe by faith in Jesus Christ, my Savior and healer! Amen.

Journal Highlights and Thoughts throughout This Process

3 DAY

Read Isaiah 35:4 (NIV)

Say to those with fearful hearts, "Be strong, do not fear; your God will come, He will come with vengeance; with divine retribution He will come to save you."

Prayer: I will no longer give in to fear. God is for me, and He will rescue me from anxiety. In the name of Jesus. Amen!

Journal Highlights and Thoughts throughout This Process

4 DAY

Read Psalm 56:3 (NIV)

When I am afraid, I put my trust in you.

Prayer: God, give me grace to trust You to deliver me from all anxiety. Thank You, Jesus! Amen.

Journal Highlights and Thoughts throughout This Process

5 DAY

Read John 14:26–27 (NIV)

But the Advocate, the Holy Spirit, whom the Father will send in my name, will teach you all things and will remind you of everything I have said to you. Peace I leave with you; my peace I give you. I do not give to you as the world gives. Do not let your hearts be troubled and do not be afraid.

Prayer: I shall live free of anxiety and declare the works of the Lord. Thank You, God, for setting me free. Amen.

Journal Highlights and Thoughts throughout This Process

6 DAY

Read Philippians 4:6–7 (NIV)

Do not be anxious about anything, but in every situation, by prayer and petition, with thanksgiving, present your requests to God. And the peace of God, which transcends all understanding, will guard your hearts and your minds in Christ Jesus.

Prayer: Father God, let Your peace fill me up so that anxiety will have to give way to Your peace. Amen!

Journal Highlights and Thoughts throughout This Process

Read 1 John 4:18 (NIV)

There is no fear in love. But perfect love drives out fear, because fear has to do with punishment. The one who fears is not made perfect in love.

Prayer: Father God, I receive Your love that will expel fear. I pray in faith that I am no longer a slave to fear. In Jesus's name I pray. Amen!

Journal Highlights and Thoughts throughout This Process

10 DAY

Read 1 Peter 5:6–7 (NIV)

Humble yourselves, therefore, under God's mighty hand, that he may lift you

up in due time. Cast all your anxiety on Him because He cares for you.

Prayer: Thank You, Father God, for delivering me from anxiety. I praise You for caring for me

in such a great way. I surrender to You and Your will. Be exulted in my life. Amen.

Journal Highlights and Thoughts throughout This Process

11 DAY

Read 1 Samuel 16:7 (NIV)

But the Lord said to Samuel, "Do not consider his appearance or his height, for I have rejected him. The Lord does not look at the things people look at. People look at the outward appearance, but the Lord looks at the heart."

Prayer: Heavenly Father, help me to see You as You see me so that I will not be anxious about anything. Amen!

Journal Highlights and Thoughts throughout This Process

12 DAY

Read Proverbs 11:18 (NIV)

A wicked person earns deceptive wages, but the one who sows righteousness

reaps a sure reward.

Prayer: God, I thank You that I am the righteousness of Jesus Christ, who heals me from all

transgressions, trespasses, inequities, and sin. Amen.

Journal Highlights and Thoughts throughout This Process

13 DAY

Read Proverbs 12:25 (NIV)

Anxiety weighs down the heart, but a kind word cheers it up.

Prayer: God, You are the keeper of my heart, and I will rest in Your promises by faith. In Jesus's name. Amen.

Journal Highlights and Thoughts throughout This Process

14 DAY

Read Proverbs 29:25 (NIV)

Fear of man will prove to be a snare, but whoever trusts in the Lord is kept safe.

Prayer: Lord, give me a healthy fear of You, and deliver me from the fear of humankind. Amen.

Journal Highlights and Thoughts throughout This Process

15 DAY

Read Psalm 23:4 (NIV)

Even though I walk through the darkest valley, I will fear no evil, for you are
with me; Your rod and your staff, they comfort me.

Prayer: God, thank You for protecting and keeping me always. You are my shepherd, and I
praise You. Amen.

Journal Highlights and Thoughts throughout This Process

16 DAY

Read Psalm 94:19 (NIV)

When anxiety was great within me, your consolation brought me joy.

Prayer: Father God, Your joy gives me strength. Thank You for overflowing joy. I received joy by faith in Jesus's name. Amen.

Journal Highlights and Thoughts throughout This Process

17 DAY

Read Psalm 27:1 (NIV)

The Lord is my light and my salvation whom shall I fear? The Lord is the stronghold of my life. Of whom shall I be afraid?

Prayer: Heavenly Father, You are stronghold of my life, and I will not fear. Amen.

Journal Highlights and Thoughts throughout This Process

18 DAY

Read Psalm 55:22 (NIV)

Cast your cares on the Lord and He will sustain you; He will never let the righteous be shaken.

Prayer: I will not be shaken, because Your righteous right hand is on me. You are the keeper of my life, and I thank and praise You. Amen.

Journal Highlights and Thoughts throughout This Process

19 DAY

Read Psalm 46:1 (NIV)

God is our refuge and strength, an ever-present help in trouble.

Prayer: God, I praise You for helping me always. Amen.

Journal Highlights and Thoughts throughout This Process

20 DAY

Read Psalm 118:6–7 (NIV)

The Lord is with me; I will not be afraid. What can mere mortals do to me? The Lord is with me; He is my helper. I look in triumph on my enemies.

Prayer: In the name of Jesus, my enemies are scattered, and anxiety is no longer.

Journal Highlights and Thoughts throughout This Process

Read Psalm 34:4–7 (NIV)

I sought the Lord, and He answered me; He delivered me from all my fears.
Those who look to Him are radiant; their faces are never covered with shame.
This poor man called, and the Lord heard him; He saved him out of all his
troubles. The angel of the Lord encamps around those who fear Him, and He
delivers them.

Prayer: God, I thank You for delivering me from all my enemies.

Journal Highlights and Thoughts throughout This Process

22 DAY

Read Joshua 1:9 (NIV)

Have I not commanded you? Be strong and courageous. Do not be afraid; do

not be discouraged, for the Lord your God will be with you wherever you go.

Prayer: In the name of Jesus, I will be strong and courageous. I will obey Your commandments.

O God, I will put my trust in You. I take authority in the name of Jesus over fear. No longer

will anxiety paralyze me; it is broken. In Jesus's name. Amen.

Journal Highlights and Thoughts throughout This Process

23 DAY

Read Matthew 6:34 (NIV)

Therefore, do not worry about tomorrow, for tomorrow will worry about itself.

Each day has enough trouble of its own.

Prayer: O God, morning by morning Your mercies are new, and great is Your faithfulness toward me. I thank You. Amen.

Journal Highlights and Thoughts throughout This Process

24 DAY

Read Deuteronomy 31:6 (NIV)

Be strong and courageous. Do not be afraid or terrified because of them, for

the Lord your God goes with you; He will never leave you nor forsake you.

Prayer: Heavenly Father, Your grace is enough to see me through. You're my strength; therefore,

I will not be afraid. In Jesus's name. Amen.

Journal Highlights and Thoughts throughout This Process

25 DAY

Read Galatians 6:7 (NIV)

Do not be deceived: God cannot be mocked. A man reaps what he sows.

Prayer: Lord, help me not to be deceived. Deliver me where I am. Search me, O Lord, and renew the right spirit within me. Amen.

Journal Highlights and Thoughts throughout This Process

26 DAY

Read Luke 6:37 (NIV)

Do not judge and you will not be judged. Do not condemn, and you will not be condemned. Forgive, and you will be forgiven.

Prayer: Father God, thank You for forgiving me. I choose to walk in forgiveness as You have forgiven me. Amen.

Journal Highlights and Thoughts throughout This Process

27 DAY

Read Luke 6:38 (NIV)

Give, and it will be given to you. A good measure, pressed down, shaken together and running over, will be poured into your lap. For with the measure you use, it will be measured to you.

Prayer: Jesus, I thank You for giving to me life in abundance and grace. As I receive from You, I give to others. Amen.

Journal Highlights and Thoughts throughout This Process

28 DAY

Read Luke 12:26 (NIV)

Since you cannot do this very little thing, why do you worry about the rest?

Prayer: I give You all that concerns me. O Lord, keep me from worrying, and teach me to trust You with all and to leave all at the foot of the cross. Amen.

Journal Highlights and Thoughts throughout This Process

29 DAY

Read Galatians 5:22–23 (NIV)

But the fruit of the Spirit is love, joy, peace, forbearance, kindness, goodness, faithfulness, gentleness and self-control. Against such things there is no law.

Prayer: Holy Spirit, fill me with the fruit of the Spirit. Be glorified in my life and cause my life to praise You. Amen.

Journal Highlights and Thoughts throughout This Process

30 DAY

Read Romans 5:8 (NIV)

But God demonstrates his own love for us in this: while we were still sinners, Christ died for us.

Prayer: I receive all You have done for me. Take all of me, and make me more like You. Amen.

Read Mark 4:39–40 (NIV)

He got up, rebuked the wind and said to the waves, "Quiet! Be still!" Then the wind died down and it was completely calm. He said to his disciples, "Why are you so afraid? Do you still have no faith?"

Prayer: I will not be afraid, because You are with me, heavenly Father. Help my unbelief in Jesus's name. Amen.

Read Mark 6:50 (NIV)

Because they all saw him and were terrified. Immediately He spoke to them and said, "Take courage! It is I. Don't be afraid."

Prayer: God, You are my help. I will take courage in You today. Amen.

Read Mark 12:33 (NIV)

To love Him with all your heart, with all your understanding and with all your strength, and to love your neighbor as yourself is more important than all burnt offerings and sacrifices.

Prayer: Heavenly Father, give me grace to love and believe You with all my heart. Amen.

Journal Highlights and Thoughts throughout This Process

Congratulations! You made it through!

Closing Prayer

God, I choose to live a healed life. I now receive a new heart that is free of emotional pain and anxiety. I am free of anxiety to love as You love and command us to love. I am special, lovable, and valuable. I am open to receiving love from others because of Your great love. By Your stripes, I am healed of anxiety.

Heavenly Father, increase my faith to believe. Help my unbelief. I pray all these in the mighty name of Jesus Christ. Amen.

You Are not Lone

Sample Suggestions for Meal Planning

Everything in moderation. Use honey as a substitute for

sugar, and be aware of your food allergies.

Increase vegetables, sprouts, fruits, and water in your diet.

Consume less drinks with sugar/fructose/corn syrup, and flour and dairy products.

Plan your meals, and buy according to your plan.

Try not to eat after 6:00 p.m.

Look into the sixteen-day fast to see if it's right for you. See your

doctor before fasting if you're taking medications.

Day 1

Breakfast

- a cup of hot water with a wedge of lemon or a bottle of water (Wait fifteen to thirty minutes before eating or drinking anything else.)
- a cup of coffee or tea
- one cup of fruit (berries, banana) with low-fat yogurt
- boiled egg

Lunch

- salad of mixed greens, goat cheese, pecans, and beets with your favorite dressing or vinaigrette and oil
- a cup of soup or green tea (hot or cold)

Dinner

- sweet potato
- baked chicken or salmon
- mixed green vegetables

Dessert

- four frozen grapes or assorted fruit dipped in chocolate syrup

Day 2

Breakfast

- spinach omelet

- cup of mixed berries

- two peeled oranges or fresh-squeezed orange juice (Avoid the concentrated juices.)

- eight ounces of water

Snack

- handful of nuts

Lunch

- cup of vegetable or lentil soup

- leafy green salad

- eight ounces of water

- turkey sandwich with tomatoes and avocados

Dinner

- half-cup brown rice

- grilled chicken breast with mango or tomatoes, salsa

- eight ounces of water or herb tea, preferably with no sugar

- half-cup asparagus

Dessert

- oatmeal cookies or a scoop of ice cream

Day 3

Breakfast

- cereal with nuts, barley, berries, and bananas, or coconut (either hot or cold)
- assorted fruits
- boiled egg
- eight ounces of water

Snack

- tea (see "Food/Supplement" list)
- a scone or a handful of nuts/fruit

Lunch

- mixed vegetables in butter sauce or your favorite dressing
- fish from the "Food/Supplement" list or your favorite
- eight ounces of water
- tea (hot or cold)
- dark chocolate (small amount)

Dinner

- an acorn squash, baked or boiled
- turkey breast
- caesar salad
- eight ounces of water or tea

Dessert

- any of your favorites (Today you are free to choose.)

Never give in to Anxiety
You are more than conquerors
Only Believe!

Resource Links

In addition to committing to the thirty-day plan to overcoming anxiety in this book, I recommend a personal assessment to help you to get to know the real you. Here are a few tools that I use in my practice. They can help you to discover your full God-given potential to live in abundant health.

- People Skills Series: This series helps you to identify your personality type and learn how to interact with people of different personality types in a healthy way.
- Arno Profile System-Temperament: The wider the gap between temperament and actual behavior, the greater the individual's anxiety levels. This will help to close the gap and help you approach life with a healthy outlook and acceptance of how wonderfully you were created.
- Myers-Briggs Type Indicator (MBTI)
- Ministry through Biblical Healing and Freedom with Prayer and the Word of God

References

Barnes, Vicki. *The Real You.*

Ritchie, Hannah, and Max Roser. 2018 - "Mental Health". Published online at OurWorldInData. org. Retrieved from: 'https//ourworldindata.org/mental-health' [online Resource]

Mayo Clinic Foundation for Medical Education and Research, 1998–2018. https://www.mayoclinic.org/diseases-conditions/generalized-anxiety-disorder/symptoms-causes/syc-20360803.

https://www.medicalnewstoday.com/articles/323454.

NIMH (2009–2018 Calm Clinics).

Psychology Today. 2016.

http://adaa.org.

https://www.glorifiedbodiesfitness.com/.

About the Author

 **Marie L. Lawson** is the founder of Prepared Approach Christian Counseling Practice in Englewood Cliffs, New Jersey. Prior to becoming a Christian counselor, she worked in the corporate world serving Fortune 100 companies for more than fifteen years. On recognizing her call to Christian counseling, she obtained her license to serve others compassionately with an ear bent toward God for direction and wisdom on behalf of those needing direction, clarification, or resolution. In her ten years of counseling, she has seen the goodness of God in situations that have involved abuse, divorce, and other serious matters where God's wisdom, love, and healing have resulted in life-changing results.

Printed in the United States
By Bookmasters